© Fiona Curran

The Hail Mary Pass

© *All copyrights remain with the author*

First Edition

ISBN 1-903110-41-6

Cover design by

Owen Benwell

**Published in 2005 by
Wrecking Ball Press
24 CAVENDISH SQUARE • HULL • ENGLAND • HU3 1SS**

# The Hail Mary Pass

Fiona Curran

**Wrecking Ball Press**

## Acknowledgements

. . . . .are due to the following magazines:

Aesthetica, Coffee House Poetry, Contains Small Parts – UEA Creative Writing Anthology, Electric Acorn, Envoi, Interpreter's House, Lamport Court, The Magazine, Moodswing, Orbis, Plinth, The Reater, The Shop, The Slab, Staple, Understanding, The Wolf.

## Thanks

The Speed-Dial Ten & Shane Rhodes

**Author's Note**

The Hail Mary pass is an American football term. It is used when a ball is thrown blind in the vague hope a receiver will make the catch and deliver a last minute victory.

This book is dedicated to the memory of
Bill Curran & Bill Stair,
men of unwavering faith.

# contents

I'm Not Gonna Make It ..................................................... 11

Once Seen ....................................................................... 12

Forefather ....................................................................... 13

Long Song ....................................................................... 14

Steve's Slip ..................................................................... 16

A Routine Procedure ..................................................... 17

Dartmoor ......................................................................... 18

You Shall Have Your Renown ....................................... 20

The Rites ......................................................................... 21

Charred ........................................................................... 22

Jazz Lover ....................................................................... 23

Home Cooking II ............................................................ 24

Blue In Green ................................................................. 25

The Undertaking ............................................................ 26

At My Hands .................................................................. 27

The Hail Mary Pass ....................................................... 28

Pillow Lover ................................................................... 29

A Little Black Thing ...................................................... 30

The Shift ......................................................................... 31

The Technology Of Modern Romance ........................ 32

Timepiece ....................................................................... 33

Body Parts ...................................................................... 34

Mother's Roses .............................................................. 37

Three Quarter Lunacy ................................................... 38

Kissing The Void ............................................................ 39

# contents

Underdogs .................................................................. 40

How She Resonates ................................................... 42

Sensory Sweep .......................................................... 43

Proustian Moment ..................................................... 44

Dark Continent .......................................................... 45

Urbanites ................................................................... 46

The Check Up ........................................................... 47

What We Suspect Is Stone ........................................ 48

Today Is The Tomorrow You Were Promised Yesterday ............ 49

Crash Position ........................................................... 50

Origami Soundtrack .................................................. 51

You Are Here ............................................................ 52

# I'm Not Gonna Make It

Cries the new superhero Joe Ordinary,
fingernails bending and the third rail underfoot.

Gasps the mountaineer, oxygen starved
blood clotting as he grapples with all forms of descent.

Whispers faith's fear, the worthy disciple
commanded to walk on the water.

Groans the leader of The-One-True-Party
as votes convert from red to blue.

Said the suicidal teenager, snipping wires,
his ex-girlfriend chained and hostage.

Thinks the woman watching her new lover
eye up another. Potential is all.

Yells the man who leaps from the fire,
his only chance, the blanket of humanity below.

Screams the soldier, a bullet in the stomach
and the medic who seals his death warrant
later becomes a poet, dies,
dangling at the end of his own creation.

## Once Seen

He believes what he saw on the central line, eastbound
that Thursday. Me, dark haired woman reading the F.T.
you, jacket bulging, briefcase scrabbling, late man,
late for work he means. That's what it says in a column squeezed
between lonely hearts and cheap long haul fights to heaven.
Wants to have lunch, a smart sushi, to finger my red lapels,
paint on me, his blank canvas, projections of commuter lust,
cast his eyes like a net over my city kissed jewels.
Lunch is his euphemism for furtive winter afternoons
in dust filled hotel rooms, where the doors never lock properly
and the blankets are thin. If I could only picture something,
the wipe of your smile, the cut of your jaw, the cast of your skin,
you might have a chance, self-interested stranger,
but I see only empty glasses here and there. So I will pass.

# Forefather

The crow examines the road kill
is it one of its own? Is it fresh enough
to snap down the gullet
a morsel to alleviate what gnaws.
But no swirling aftermath here,
the steady march of maggots
willing to unburden the bones
are absent from this gentle creature,
a storm-torn umbrella, gutted,
skeletal spokes bared in accusation.
Crushed into the verge, its imprint
the wing of a baby pterodactyl
from which the crow has deduced
its direct descent.

## Long Song

And there she is.  He's kept an eye on her and her fat pal,
taking turns on the circuit that separates the wallflower
from the floor show, the circling of the booted and suited
expands and contracts with a chemical buzz.
Cool as able, he retreats to the bar, the swinging hips
and casual grind viewed through the promenade,
a giant spinning tachyscope, turning the dancers
moot sophistication crude, animating reality,
the brass effect, a lovers jerk.

There's been a few other girls, he's heading for status
of boy of the world, but none quite like her
and he can't put a finger on it, it's not in the tidy legs
or the cut of her ultra modern mane,
the smoking brown eyes laced with soot,
not even in those lovely tits, generous,
post war;  If he's a lucky duck, much later on,
they wont turn out to be a cotton wool creation,
if he's seriously lucky.

Fellow apprentices line the bar in various stages
of Saturday night's given, he's too sober still,
not enough pills and swill to make him buoyant,
bob on the sea of boppers, another pint of mild
might keep the fighting spirit up, toes tap regardless
of boring bloody Dusty.  Then cord by magic cord,
that blue, blues intro, a gauntlet and we're off,
a wave of blokes wash across the floor,
in a flood of frisky promise because

Tonight, The Animals, God bless R & B, wail the longest song.
Four and a half minutes, the luxury of time enough
to make all your mistakes and right them again,
for hands to slip and stay uncorrected
ear lobes flicked by randy tongues and a little light body pressing,
just to let her know your packing, a hint no more,
some lasses don't care for even a hint right off
just the odd chaste kiss, then you know it's courtship full
and possibly ever lasting.

What will he get from his black eyed girl?
Her name she tries to politely shout, little Evie
and her man child, the serpent sharp with apple
or without, as the last swell of Eric's anguish
dies and The Temptations beat fills the air,
couples couple, bodies twist and split the floor
still her hand rests on his shoulder, one long song down,
all night, all night, can he keep her all night,
can he keep her even one song more?

# Steve's Slip

| Race/Event | Odds |
|---|---|
| Chances of backing another second place | 2/1 |
| "    "    getting a decent horse off Jim | 10/1 |
| "    "    backing another winner | 18/1 |
| "    "    incurring the wrath of wife if he hits the pub | Evens |
| "    "    getting a decent meal out of the bitch tonight | 20/1 |
| "    "    there being a beer in the fridge | 33/1 |
| "    "    friday night hanky-panky (If winnings transferred to wife) | 40/1 |
| "    "    a shag, without transfer to the above | 80/1 |
| "    "    breakfast in bed | 100/1 |
| "    "    not spending the weekend ferrying his snotty kids, seeing the Monster-in-Law, or visiting B&Q | 500/1 |
| "    "    being happy with his lot ever again | No Odds Quoted |

Book Closed.

# A Routine Procedure

Rolling along, the gurney groaning, sicker than I,
the crumbling ceiling stretching back into infinity,
I am on the way to have you removed.
All other treatments have failed, even the Benzedrine and booze,
I could pass you naturally since pain is in fashion,
but all the complimentary cures at my disposal
are poor substitute for the precision of the scalpel.

Doors flap and slap and I am swiftly prepared;
but unprepared always for the hollow this tumour,
as old as an imagined son will leave. Nurses tut,
a minor infection, but when they open me up
the surgeon gasps at the sight of so much scar tissue,
the state of the valves. He does his best, but all agree it's futile.

*All gone*, the Sister soothes, her hands clammy with lies,
*Success*, but the body echoes where they prised you out
wrenched you from me, another vital chunk junked
*Couldn't you have been more careful?* I want to shout
*When you ripped the last of my lovers out?*

# Dartmoor

Relieved of the need to interpret sign or quality
I take a run at the rock,
the Tor at the tip of this moor
reduces me to kid or ram;
I bound Tenzing style to the summit
and look down at green ungraded.
King of the castle
my court clothes flags in the wind,
signalling residency but not command
over the edges of a land
that even the Romans left uncharted.

Winded, afraid to fall, I lay down
and embrace the rock,
celebrate my insignificance,
swallowed like a morsel on a seismic plate
a digested detail in God's plan.

God's plan? Too overawed I sprout hooves,
scrabble where there's no stone loose
and bask in cloud break.
Here my kin, the wily ram looks over blankly
comprehends the uncomprehending,
returns to what is his
knowing my survival here is unlikely.
But not this alpine. A livid blotch
obstinate on the rock, small spiny blooms
barely ruffled by the elemental blur,
its splash of Chelsea colour surprises me,
defeats with rough beauty. A last consideration
before retirement of the deity.

Dog ends snarl in pockets,
afraid to leave the smallest mark
I troop through ferns to the Tor's size ten foot.
The first people encountered an eye sore,
as if on the apex I had been transformed
back into base building blocks, particles,
the ripe promise of the prototype.
A predecessor on the flint road to humanity.

## You Shall Have Your Renown

Coming here to work an escape,
leafing through a stack of old film books,
I found you disguised as David Hemmings
that cruel photographer in "Blow Up".
Are you happy now my darling?
Knowing my heart has already cast you,
made you into a movie star,
beauteous and untouchable.

# The Rites

We crawl by, photographing you, the bad accident,
something everyone slows to see.  We all do.
Still alive your crocus shoot fingers poke through soil
fit for cattle and crow alone.  If I grasped
your green hand, would a tug of war ensue?
You'd have me down there with you
and I momentarily willing – that is respect for you,
there would be none for me, bitch, rival, even whore.

But darling had you seen death before you did it?
The aftermath of the Reapers work,
skin mottled purple when the blood settles
in arse, back, elbows.  Cold?
Because the fire in the lungs has popped its last crackle.
Those we love die with morphine eyes open,
they glaze before fingers ripple lashes shut,
the body vacates, the smell, a final letting go.

Then we wash, wash away, prepare for dust,
absolve the shell in all its paper frailty.
Resting the body sideways, then sideways,
the winding sheet falling into a fold above the heart,
a clean white blossom pressed to the breast:
Then the spirit risen and cloudy as steam
discovers its weightlessness, shouts, *'result, result!'*
slamming the door on its way out.

# Charred

Shocking how we never took.
Even after smoke signals galore
and bellows fanned our lust,
even aided with accelerants and poker force
a broadsheet acting as the doors,
we seemed to pass through
the well stoked flame and go
from smouldering to embers.

Unsurprising with your wife
burning white with fury.
She holds all the matches.
I carbonize under crumbling coals,
the phutt of *put me out*
blistering the once kissed mouth.

## Jazz Lover

Is it Sonny or was it Monk
that said, Jazz is in the genes,
I see that now we've met,
as surely as Miles came before
and between us.  But you Coleman,
may I call you that?
Kissed me with a tenor sax tender,
hitting the pelvic dance floor
in all the right paces.
Swing day for night,
blow me in and out,
like the warm Missouri wind
which flew to your lips unaided,
when first you made a play.
Make like love to me, for today
you have replaced all others,
every Art and Bud and Charlie,
they have gone the way
of easy, pillow lovers;
And so I am devoted, gentle Hawk
to only you.  That breath,
slow, slow now Coleman,
soft draw and fill me.

## Home Cooking II

Bird Blew.
Ba
    da da da da da da da da
                          dah,
H raised him up, H scaled him
                     <u>d</u>own
A one man poly     p-h-o-n-y.
      *1234*
                  Counterpoint's beeeebop soldier,
Square bashing three deuces d<u>ow</u>n,
                <u>Off</u>
                Off the parade ground,
                        Yardbird cooking
             and MADness brewing,
play my spine from the base do<u>wn</u>
                      *(and all around)*
        Alto,
            every spine and make Jazz Jello
    *— hey*            float
                    this lady's boat
with Crazeology.

        Then thunder improvised a track
    that rolled Charlie all the way <u>back</u> to Kansas,
             back
        a little number finished way too
soon

    he blew and he blew till he blew out
                Bird Blew.

# Blue In Green

*After Miles Davis*

April 1959

At the core of it and mute
one of a million lonely insomniacs,
behind his eyes a dull red throb
                    A dupe pulls up his collar
watches the rain bounce off brown stone steps.
                    on leaving the Sandman's, a fellow insomniac
                    who helps feed the city's nasty habits.

                    Fin dented, tail light out,
                    a woman lolls unconscious on the shoulder
                    of some go figure, consumed by darkness.

                    Drenched before he reaches the wheel.
                    The engine cuts out
After rubbing his eyes    but he has the fix to fix everything,
black circles on black,    they can go now.
he watches the good tail light corner
by the neon of the old Baptist Ministry.

# The Undertaking

Remember Michael? Our Dad's undertaker and Mam's as well,
I always think of him when I go to funerals,
how he stood alone in the left hand pews, away from us at the crem.
*Why?* I whispered, and you promoted to Head of the Family said,
*He represents the Dead, he's a stand in for Dad on the other side.*
From time to time, distracted from the terrible contents of that coffin,
I would catch him out of the corner of my eye, intoning,
doing his sombre bit, looking brutally sad because he knew Dad.
And I wanted to go over and knock his hat from his hand,
drag him back to the family, tell him
*Come and sit with us again, forget death.*

## At My Hands

Freckles mutate with dangerous speed into liver spots.
Veins sit proud as speed bumps between knuckles,
joints grind trapping tendons as they flex.
Nails, a short brutality, flaws pronounced, ugly.
Rings rotate, diamonds slip and turn away
their sparkle palmed. Only a fist makes the skin smooth
like a girls.

When my young lover runs his lips
over the back of my unfaithful hands, the skin ripples.
Follicle geometric's compact into lines, the script of my life.
The epidermis slackens, the outside hanging on the in,
an ill fitting suit, that needs to be tucked
in all folding places. Surely he must see this?
The Vampire's hands

                    bled white, the undead tissue,
a papery pattern. Creation's cowboy blueprints.

## The Hail Mary Pass

Time out,
gum shield washed and reinserted
the trainer's shoulders are folded into the dug out.

Fourth quarter desperation,
the swarming defence surge like Trojans,
breached we scatter, I stumble

but do not go down.
Backward leap and from left-field
the ball rotates into my muddy hands

my fleeting responsibility–
a promise which must be air-bourne
before the next tackle.  Which is now.

Exploding on impact, mid-air,
a throw as blind as shrapnel
spins suspended in the arms of chance.

We hang in space praying for interception.
The receiver pounds head down,
I obey gravity, bones tasting ground,

head sinking. Then the tidal roar
prizing the eyes from the micro,
the eureka of understanding.

# Pillow Lover

The pillow represents you,
you and all the come and gone
the has been, will be.
When night goes to work
and sleep is as far from me
as you and all of you,
I tuck the fattest pillow
snug, into my back
and it quickly warms through.
It draws my heat, my love
into cotton and feathers
not skin. And I sigh
in the dark for the lack
of hair, hands, a face,
sigh and slowly turn to
the pillow, hold it anyway
and imagine. My love
must go somewhere.

# A Little Black Thing

Above me is my own personal cloud with no silver lining;
A black dog trots obediently at my high heel;
doubt settles on the shoulder, a cocky parrot chanting my mantra
"Fool, you fool".  My inner daemon wakes and stretches,
discuses cancer with the busy hypochondriac
knitting my intestines into something more appropriate.
My aura's the colour of London fog, blues navy.
There has been a total eclipse of the heart;
I have been disowned as the black sheep of the family.
Not content to be down in the dumps my soul's landfill.
The long day's journey into night has taken more
than a long day's journey into night.  There's no room at the inn
and purgatory's bar has become members only.
The ninth circle of hell has frozen over again
and God has declared eternity a wet August bank holiday.

The nights are fair drawin' in, love is a lottery.
On the horizon there's this little black thing.

# The Shift

What was it I said? Her name?
One minute smoking your dark, smelly cheroot
quite happily puffing and letting the blue ash rush back
to settle in drifts on your overworked olive cords;
Expression sunny, your body, as ever, an uncoiled
but friendly snake. You smiled a lot up till then,
relaxed into my unedited, anxious chatter.
Then the change, imperceptible to our friend in the back,
struggling with the map you had refused to read.
You tensed too late for the blow, a swift nasty smack
entirely delivered; and you flicked your smoke end,
snapped it brutally into the retreating road, flashing
full dying sparks. But you kept your lungs full of hate,
which you blew vigorously around the ridiculous car,
so that I might suffer with you, for you.
Then you attended to the previous ashes, brushed them
from your re-sprung legs, like bugs, disgusted.

The retreat was total, from her percussive name
and we sat an endless mile in dreadful silence.
Me knowing now, the power of her, deadly in any form;
and I tried not to watch, as you slipped the mask on,
rolling it over everything, deafening yourself to any kindness.

As our navigator ordered a sharp right at the pike,
I waited for you to form cataracts
just to be on the safe side.

# The Technology Of Modern Romance

Wont C U again
then? Charming
way 2 end it I
must say, tk
balls? Bet office
bike lined up nxt,
lucky girl. Ur
shirts R in
Oxfam. Dont txt
me ever. Bastard.

# Timepiece

My Mother's dress watch
ticks strong against the room,
against reason.

Re-gilded, hands reset,
mechanism re-calibrated
face facing fresh scratches,

but still she runs erratic.

This strapped on shell
is the echo of the big tick,
the knocking of your heart

killing time.  Mine.
Categorical it tells me, hurry,
meet your Mother

half way.

# Body Parts

**Feet**

Suddenly I noticed your feet,
how smooth and soft the heels were
poking out of the sheets, hovering
above my impatient, lonely hands.
The nurses told me, that they would sneak
and put on cream before you woke,
make the skin translucent, your instep shine.
I remember cutting your toenails before this,
remember you soaking encrusted soles,
your heels cracked like baked desert sand,
the eventual flaking skin, relief erasing
the million miles, the night shift worker
with squared off toes had done.  The ache
of the dead hours, now floating dead skin scum
ready to be drained away, the vague comfort
of flexing your toes in a soft towel,
you could believe yourself mended.
So now your feet are beautiful,
now that you cannot remember
where you walk, they will take you
uncomplaining, anywhere.
Take you in circuits through the mist,
to the end of yourself, you silently pace.

**Hands**

These days you use them mostly for food,
pinching a slice of cheap cake too hard
the only object of your desire crumbles
under a touch which has lost its subtlety.
Now they are weak liver spotted paws
nails not painted, nor manicured, as once, always.
All notions of caress have died, though sometimes
you'll hold the hand of a nurse or passing stranger.
Hold me.  Fingers do not drum, fiddle with cigarettes,
check off numbers, do not clip pearls to your ears,
smooth the Christmas dinner dress down.
They lay in your lap, on your low belly,
in my hated silence I mourn completely
their loss of expression, their strength.
Best when you pulled fresh sun-lit sheets
from the line, the tug before the fold,
baked flannel whipping out of my hands,
trailing in the dew grass, your grip too tight
and I would let go, bending to quiet retrieval.
Stroking the folds of skin below the knuckles,
in truth, I know, I do not love your harsh hands,
too many stinging slaps to my recoiling face,
unannounced.  You smile very suddenly
my shame smiles back and with open arms
you entreat me hold you, love.  Still when we touch,
inside I leap scolded from the sudden stroke
of your bloodless hand.

## Mouth

Unmanned, a last kiss, behind it
you were gone and those wet open lips
feel like the unformed, wide mouthed kiss
of an infant. Or some strange savage
who doesn't know what a kiss is.
I sponge your dry lips with tepid water,
watch the long slow pull of your chest
every breath, a rip in your lungs,
the struggle, a fifteen second gap.  More.
You who showered us with kisses
is dying.  Kissing Dad, kissing me, strong dry kisses
or tiny nibbles on a washed cheek, I think
you enjoyed kissing right down to your boots
with those Max Factor lips.  And eating
and smoking and talking, all things lips
and I am truly your daughter in this.
No more kisses blown will take flight,
manned or solo, the next will be mine alone,
terrified lips brushing pulled shut eyes,
trying to love the glued corners of your mouth,
in the defrosting coffin cold box,
never big enough for endless dreams,
all the night's lights.  Before all this
I must be here to see, lay you out, ready.
Wait.  The day opens and I kiss your top lip,
check the pulse of your breathless body,
then taking my inadequate coat, I go to smoke
a pointless cigarette in October's early ice.

## Mother's Roses

Those dried roses I have placed out of reach
but still within sight, in a champagne flute
on top of the wardrobe.

When I look at them, their once fresh stems
slip through my fingers again, sharp as the day
I plucked them, hurried from your wreath.

The red of them, even with the life burnt out
seems to me the truth of all that you are,
even dead you are life and passion

fire not frost.  Still, I imagine you in the air
enfolding me, all arms;  I imagine you
looking at the top of the wardrobe.

# Three Quarter Lunacy

It's when they ask for a pretty moon shot,
something to tart up the daring escape scene in another period drama
or some dreary Natural History thing about vanishing turtles.
Pretty how do you mean?  I want to say,
(because I already know their full moon, full face,
passing cloud over top left answer).  Which side would you like?
Pre 59 or post Luna 3?  Then the researcher will get mad
because she wants a moon plain and simple

but it doesn't come unadorned.  I look after the planets
and the moon is my baby, our little satellite,
who pulls us by our tidal coat tails
reminding us twice daily with a gravitational tantrum
that she is there.  I have seen a thousand pictures
of her good face, her pock marked sunny side
turned permanently towards us, her true self concealed
from the waiting world, until caught by Soviet Cameras.

I long to send one perfect image to these dullards,
the splendid silver tennis ball, hanging top centre
and if a hand could pass through that regular electrical field,
into the cold everlasting night of space,
draw that primeval fragment towards your heart,
feel her terrible scar tissue wrapped in gravity
soothe her bedrock self of sharp loneliness,
take pity and cradle her momentarily–

but they want the moon at the window as usual.
Shot no 73: Transforming werewolf howls at reluctant cliché.

# Kissing The Void

> For D.S.
> *The dreams in which I'm dying*
> *are the best I've ever had*
> Tears for Fears - Mad World

I felt you die last night in increments.
The sheer drop of sleep, the bone breaking abyss
holds no fears for you.  Negotiated by abseil,
rope running, glissade confined
by the bounce of boots on breaking rock–
I hear them crumble far below.
Panic spasmodic, you shudder through me
the anchor, my burning gloves are all that hold.
I love to watch you die and die again,
until the rock is gorged, a last twitch
before the mangled breathing and the slack rope.
My turn, still rich in conquest I hesitate,
the aurora glows.  Your dreams have you,
in mine I watch you sleep.

# Underdogs

*After Guy Barker*

Their soles hit the pavement with a confident leather slap, converging from all four corners, booted and suited, ready; the steady rain a pisser, a snare drum hissing solo on Soho **meanwhile** Pete's already in position, feeling as conspicuous as an albino tap-dancing in the pool of a street light, he watches for any unexpected arrival **meanwhile** Ray wakes up with the hangover to end them all and already she's yapping at him about the wasp's nest in the garden, he rolls over and faces the radio, she yanks the curtains open blinding him, he curses and little bits of last night come flooding back, including a blow job that he hopes he didn't pay for; the man says the time is ten fifteen and suddenly his heart kicks in, cymbals crash, late for his own funeral **meanwhile** Floyd throws his wife and kid out of the car under the flyover at White City, she's in one again so she can bloody well walk, like he gives a fuck. No, in a couple of hours all his troubles will be over, just pick up the flowers on Uxbridge Road and look the part mate **meanwhile** in a bar on the Walworth Road, Bill watches the clock, with only the racing to distract him, he orders another scotch, raises a toast to the lads and the day when he can retire with his dogs, forget all about this fucking cesspool London **meanwhile** Ray sits on the tube at Sloane Square willing the bastard thing to move, sweat forming rivulets on his back, he whistles 'Native Boy' through his teeth **meanwhile** up above low horns growl, the traffic crawls on Tarmac steaming after a down pour and Louis replaces another drill bit in the quiet of the vault; he's thinking about Sonia, the bronze beauty he was with Sunday night, a gorgeous girl, the colour of Spain. His probation officer rang earlier and everyone laughed, way too hard, like you do when the old adrenalin is pumping **meanwhile** a hearse pulls up round the back and a white child's casket is removed solemnly by two men, wreaths laid lovingly aside, they do not smile although they want to **meanwhile** Bill turns his mobile over in his fist, should he call a few short odds into the bookies while he's waiting? **meanwhile** Ray's luck has turned, George won't be killing him after all, because they tumble through his fingers like virgin's tears, white and yellow and his joy is inexpressible, he's well made up, Louis whacks his back, the daft bastard singing *'Diamonds are a girl's best friend'* at the top of his whorey old voice **meanwhile** through the din a distant siren sings in Pete's ears, wailing its anxious way up to Camden and he is well fucked off, should have been relieved before now by that scumbag Ray who has **meanwhile** dodged into a sex shop off Berwick Street market, to avoid bumping into his bloody sister-in-law, he can't stand that cunt and anyway what's she doing up west?  He realises his breathing is far too heavy even for a pervert, so he heads straight over to the bondage section, tries to look all interested an' that **meanwhile** five men load the little coffin into the back of the hearse, darkness spreading like a stain over the silent tableau, George plucks a flower from a heart shaped wreath, the pink, a smiling buttonhole **meanwhile** Ray

## How She Resonates

*for Attila József*

Did the dawn insist
on joie de vivre
or did the pale blue band
slowly reveal another poem?
A night watchman in a cornfield
you'd had plenty of time
in the cradle of darkness
to think of her. And when some fool
set to holy campanology
a mile or so away, you saw
clappers swaying inside bells,
the motion of her skirt and legs
love walking towards you.
You made a circuit
feeling your own legs re-animate
staggering through future hay,
while magpies steal the dense silence
that night punctuated
with a million sibilant children,
who amused themselves
by swirling her name all around you.

## Sensory Sweep

You were lavender when you passed
from the oil in the bath I had poured
which you complained had overheated you.
Purple in your terry towel, baked heather
in your attitude and drunk on some
cheap Bordeaux and elastic American prose.
And I could smell your dark intolerance
that dank musk of temper and I was
never so glad to have your measure,
as your wet feet padded damp into my rugs
and that sweet, rich coating fell away
via the half open window in the bedroom.

# Proustian Moment

Proust's Equation of 1921 clearly states:-

where Time (unqualified) is **T**
The <u>Self</u> in parallel dimensions – Past/Present/Future/($4^{th}$ excluded)
is shown (to the power of 1) as **S¹**
and memory  <u>Memory</u>  is  **<u>M</u>**  then:-
  Comprehension *(classical)*  **C**

$$T + S^1 + \frac{M}{C} = PM$$

for further clarification please refer to masterwork,
*A la recherche du temps perdu.*

## Dark Continent

Given leave to chart your continents, your global spread,
I started close to Arctic North with the eyes,
but barely took their blueness in before rushing out
and boarding Concorde. A supersonic map was required.
You passed under and through me completely
but lacked true detail. I boarded the Orient Express
but still you sped by, limbs as cameos',
torso as blank as sky, mouth a blur.
To penetrate this sharp coast line
I borrowed the Roi des Belges,
floated down tangled rivers
tracking veins to the very heart of you.
Caught at the source in Maiden's hair,
I took to my feet and walked all over you,
but you soon brought me down, cut the legs from me
and the only transport left was that of lips, the only journey,
that of teeth, of tongues, that of the night kill.

# Urbanites

The first squeezed through the bars
high tailing into the churchyard.
Second, a rust blur retreating
from the sour stink of human.
A third, swathed in bloody monochrome,
carcass swooning in its jaws
entrails confirming another local storm.

And the roads lay dead
the arse end of January, cars sporadic.
Only I was knotting paths with the new urbane;
vixens in possession,
their strange cries rippling the sky,
telling tall tales of the territories, emphatic,
this is mine, this is mine, all mine.

# The Check Up

*After Dorothy Parker*

The doctor smiles, no sign of virus
Blood count normal, haemoglobin up;
Nothing accounts for this sickness
Deathly parlour, decided lack of luck.
The file is closed; I'm neatly labelled
Hypochondriac or something worse,
No mention of what truly ails me,
You as affliction, you as curse.

# What We Suspect Is Stone

In the evening, after the bourgeois tourists, but before the cleaners, David shrugs and stretches, a perfect foot — excluding the broken toe, steps from the plinth. He sometimes slips on a floor made glass by the millions who have circled him.

He is glad of the rest, standing there all day, representing truth and beauty, the epitome of Art. It's a struggle at times though he makes it look easy. Hard to believe he was once an awkward block shrouded with pitted cloth, but he remembers emerging, the adrenaline and the heart beating under what we suspect is stone. His creator's beaded brow. Then himself, the curls and the fierce eye, the juvenile biceps ready to power the sling, he'll save his people alright if he can just get the rest of this rock off his back. Be fully hewn at last.

The Slaves moan, unfinished they call out to him, usually he feels their sorrow, they talk, but tonight the boy king wants to relax, lay down and replay his latest victory. Turn over in his mind the awe struck crowd, the women orbiting his heavenly body, examining every nook and cranny, their lust still pleases him even after centuries. His imperfections he knows only serve his humanity. The cleaners will have to work round him he decides, rolling on to his back, wishing the Sistine ceiling was above.

And he is not alone. All around the world lovers unfurl and cease to kiss, emaciated stick men dangle their pins and crushed bodies open their arms to strength. Dancers drop their pirouettes, even the embodiment of antiquity, those without heads, limbs, rest and recline. Birds in space fly. Eyes revert to that generous painted nude. Every statue breathes solitude.

## Today Is The Tomorrow You Were Promised Yesterday
*t.m. Victor Burgin*

```
              M.O.M.A.    NYC.
           11 West 53rd Street
           New York, NY 10019.


    Pollock Coasters           $   6.99
    Hepworth Paperweight       $  35.00
    Dali Clock Cuff-links      $  17.99
    Waterlilies T-Towel        $   9.00
    Koons Toy Poodle           $  14.99
    Bacon Triptych Fridge M    $   5.50
    Warhol Campbell's Pen      $   4.00
    Hirst Shark Choc           $   8.00
    Schiele Sex Manual         $  70.00


    Subtotal                   $171.47
    Tax                        $   3.46

    TOTAL                      $174.93


    CARD NUMBER
    ************6941
    EXPIRY DATE/0602
    VISA DELTA/Sale            $174.93

    5/14/02    14.16

              Please Retain This Receipt
                 M.O.M.A.    NYC.
                    Thank You
                 HAVE A NICE DAY
```

# Crash Position

In the event of heartbreak
remember that your every instinct told you so,
labelled him most wanted, a terrorist
casually carrying a chemical weapon,
deadly secretions detonate on target,
the blush on your skin tells you so.

Bomber command, duty bound,
watch you nose-dive on the radar,
have stopped coding their signals, beg you,
*Put the boy down! Do not tinker*
*with that which is taking you lovingly apart,*
*we'll never put you back together.*
Fuel warning light ignored,
you watch the bolts in the fuselage pop,
glass crack, the pressure drop,
it's a disaster, and every time he leaves
you assume crash position.

# Origami Soundtrack

She reminds me, Lauren, my neighbour's two year old;
her laugh already dirty, developing, I can hear her teenage future
through these tissue walls.  Walls pull at the ears, barking dogs,
babies with perfect pitch, television, scooters, sex,
the odd brutal domestic, planes escaping overhead.
Eavesdrop on me and the solo melody
is the self importance of paper, books, manuscripts,
the stuff you have to hand; I rustle and sometimes emit music.
In that near silence even my inner walls ring, I'm jerry-built,
the womb vacant still, while cracks in the mind
let strange ideas slip on to paper, that I despise then crush.
I justify these abortions to my unborn teenage daughter
who's having none of it, screams she doesn't understand,
smoothing each disaster out with the heel of her hand.

## You Are Here

The red dot orientate's,
situates you in the context of the map.
On the arc, the A to Z of yourself
you have only the cardinal points; children mark time,
but what about wisdom, the articles of faith,
how do we know when we have arrived at love?
Achieved colour, a Seurat dot amongst others.
Standing under the map, being here
roots you momentarily. *You are here*
you say to a man and his son,
in a language not their own
pointing to the dot. *And you,* you cry,
arms open to the tens, the thousands,
*are here*, every strobing arc tangible,
electric, each route bisecting static air.